Copyright © 2018 by Gahmya Drummond-Bey.

All rights reserved.

Published by Evolved Teacher Press.

No part of this publication may be reproduced, stored,
or transmitted in any form or by any means,
electronic, mechanical, photocopying,
recording, scanning, or otherwise, except as permitted
under Section 107 or 108 of the 1976 United States Copyright Act,
without the prior written permission of the author.
Requests to the author and publisher for
permission should be addressed to the
following email: gahmya@kidyouniversity.com

Limitation of liability/disclaimer of warranty: While the publisher and
author have used their best efforts in preparing this guide and
workbook, they make no representations or warranties with
respect to the accuracy or completeness of the contents of this
document and specifically disclaim any implied warranties
of merchantability or fitness for particular purpose.
No warranty may be created or extended by sales
representatives, promoters, or written sales materials.

Due to the dynamic nature of the Internet, certain links and website information
contained in this publication may have changed.
The author and publisher make no representations to the current
accuracy of the web information shared.

Today is an awesome day when little minds and tiny fingers begin to show the world how amazing it is when they work together. This writing book was created by an American educator and taught in South Korea for at least eight years before being used globally! Children from the ages of 5 to 9 have all used this same book and have been inspired to love writing. Today's children are extremely intelligent and they are initially motivated to write with this book because it acknowledges just how brilliant they are! But, there's more! Along with this writing guide, you also receive a code for the animated course!

It's amazing what a child can do if someone believes in them! When this belief is added to a bit of fun art and topics of interests, amazing results are produced.

To the adult who sees this and thinks, "My kid could never do that," just try! Kids are spectacular!

www.kidYOUniversity.com

The Animated Course

Be sure to sign up for the super engaging animated course that accompanies this workbook! Dive in here:
www.evolvedteacher.com/favorite

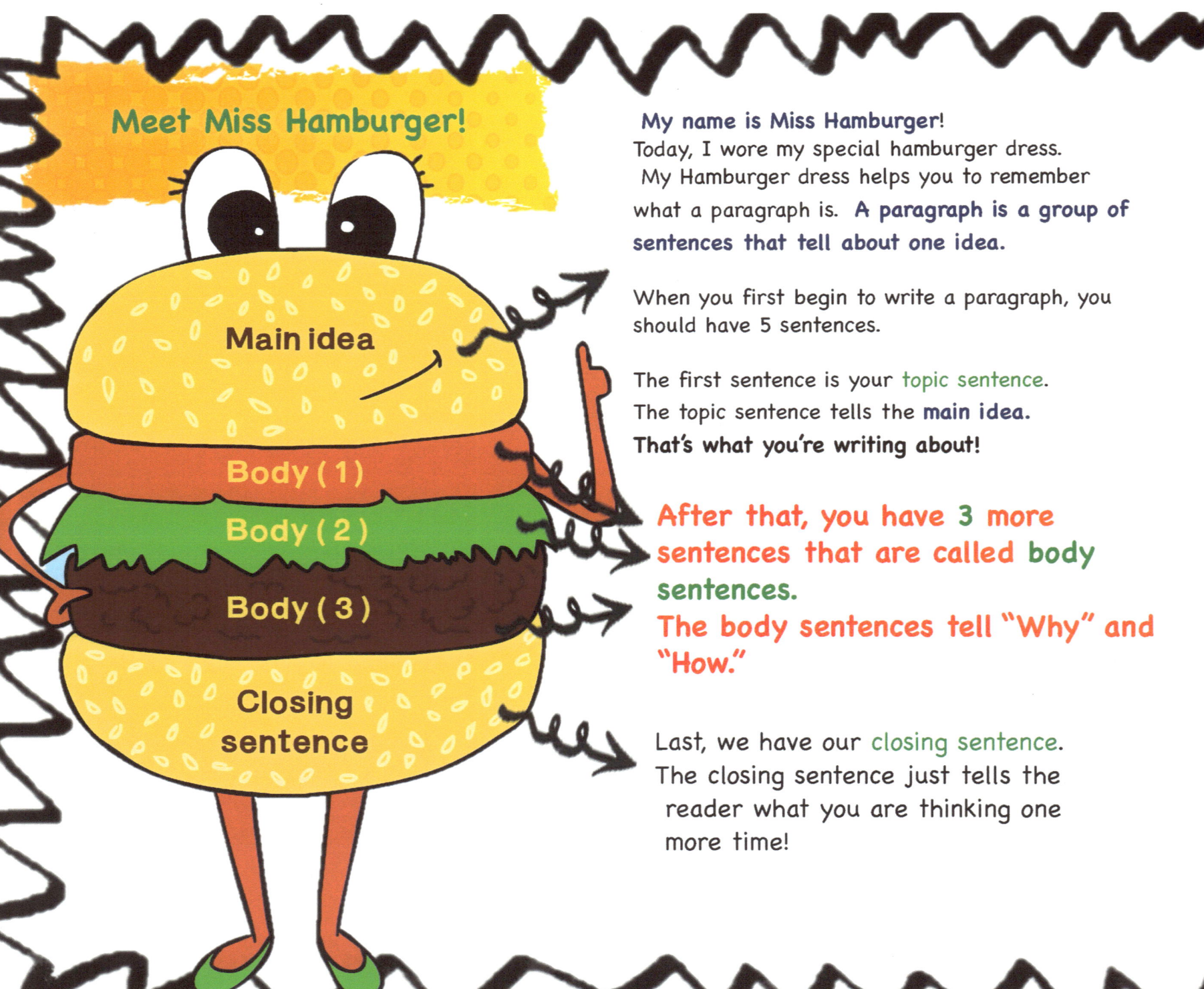

Meet Miss Hamburger!

- Main idea
- Body (1)
- Body (2)
- Body (3)
- Closing sentence

My name is Miss Hamburger! Today, I wore my special hamburger dress. My Hamburger dress helps you to remember what a paragraph is. **A paragraph is a group of sentences that tell about one idea.**

When you first begin to write a paragraph, you should have 5 sentences.

The first sentence is your topic sentence. The topic sentence tells the **main idea**. **That's what you're writing about!**

After that, you have 3 more sentences that are called body sentences. The body sentences tell "Why" and "How."

Last, we have our closing sentence. The closing sentence just tells the reader what you are thinking one more time!

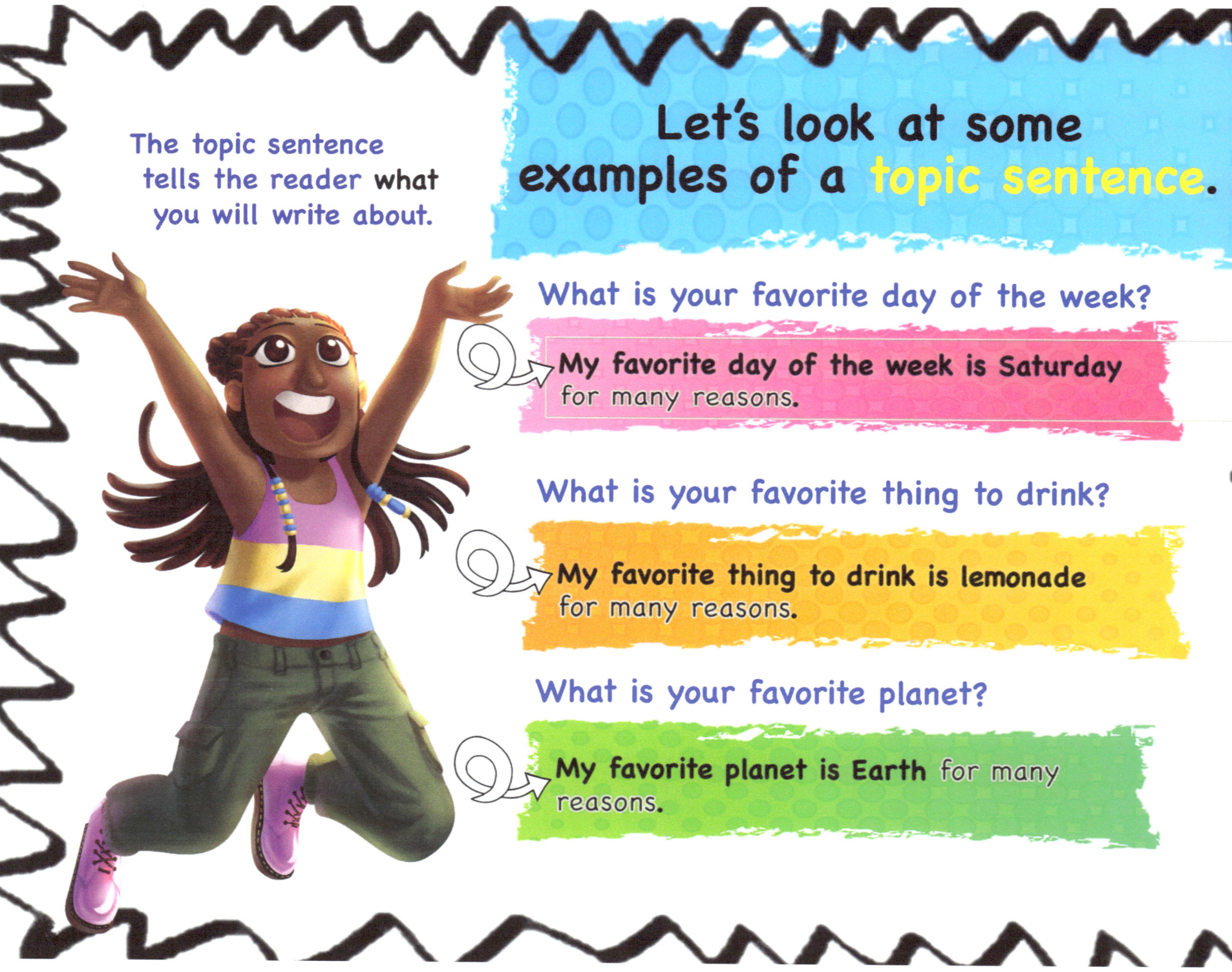

TOPIC SENTENCES

3 What is your favorite food?

_____

_____

4 What is your favorite toy?

_____

_____

5 What is your favorite movie?

_____

_____

Table of Contents

 1. What is your favorite holiday?

 2. What is your favorite color?

 3. What is your favorite animal?

 4. What is your favorite season?

 5. What is your favorite sport?

 6. What is your favorite fruit?

 7. What is your favorite dessert?

 8. What is your favorite body part?

 9. What is your favorite day of the week?

 10. What is your favorite instrument?

 11. What is your favorite cartoon character?

 12. Who is your best friend?

 13. Who is your favorite teacher?

 14. Who is your favorite person?

 15. Celebration Time!

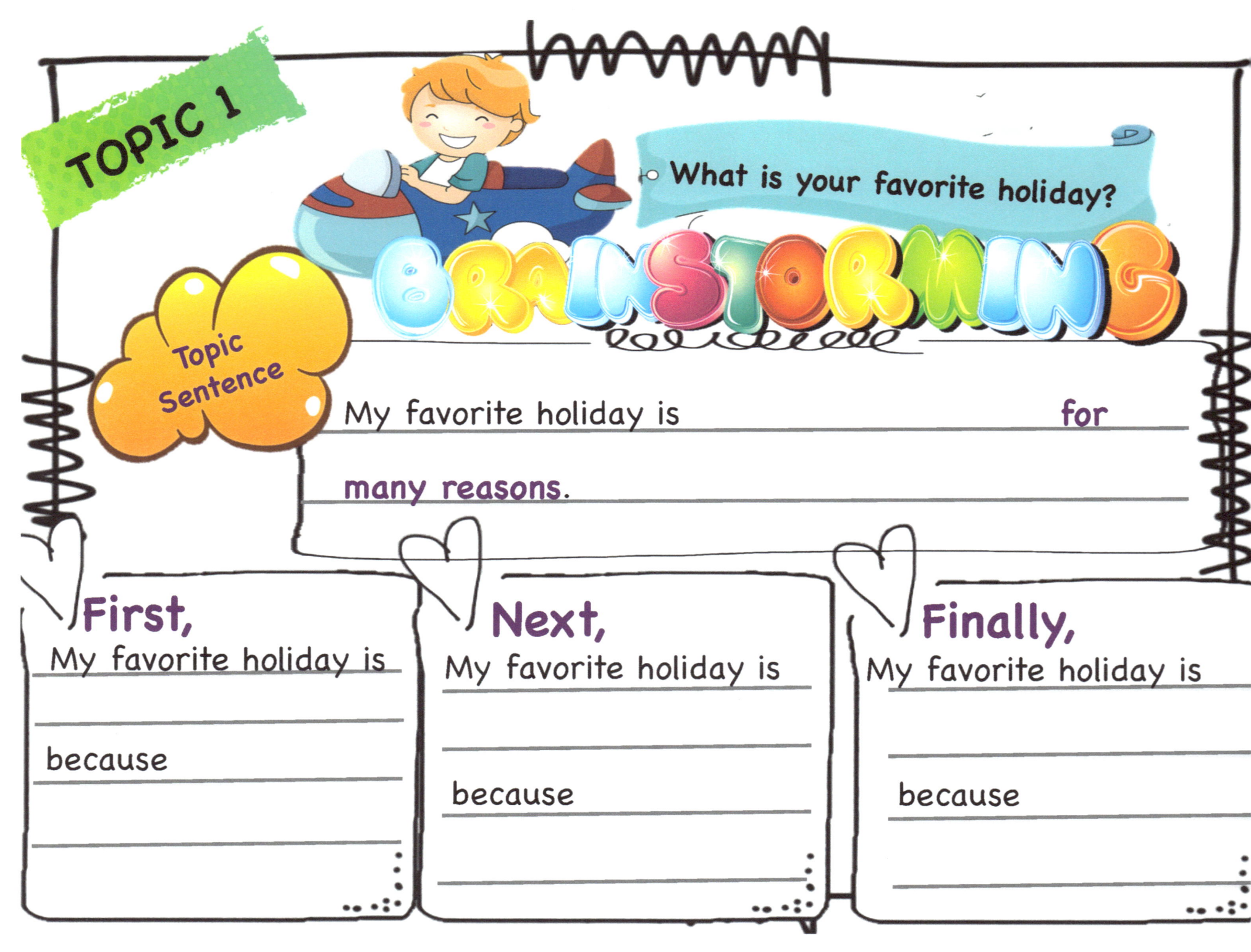

TOPIC 1

Use your paragraph to draw pictures.
(Show each of your reasons.)

FIRST,

NEXT,

FINALLY,

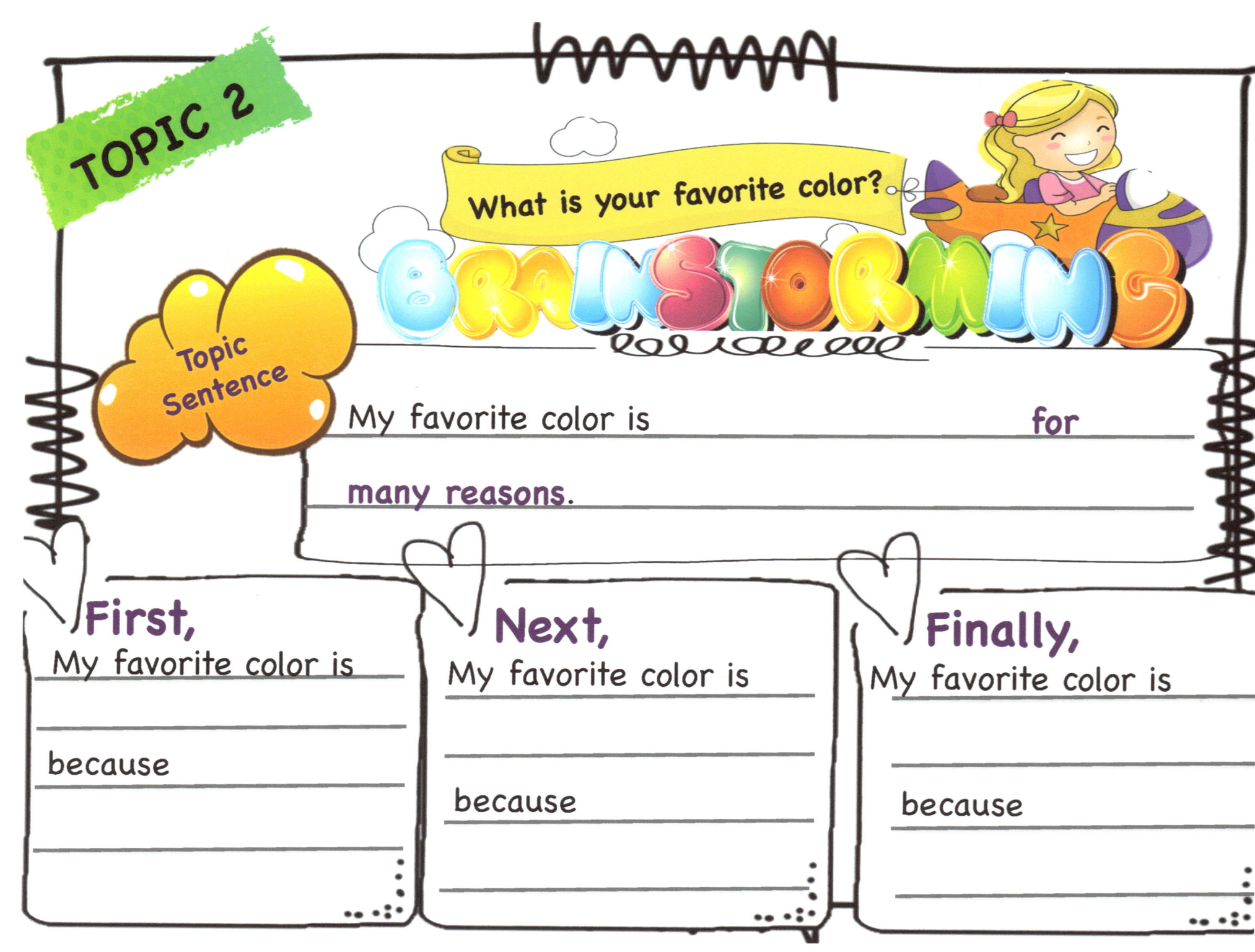

TOPIC 2

Use your paragraph to draw pictures.
(Show each of your reasons.)

FIRST,

NEXT,

FINALLY,

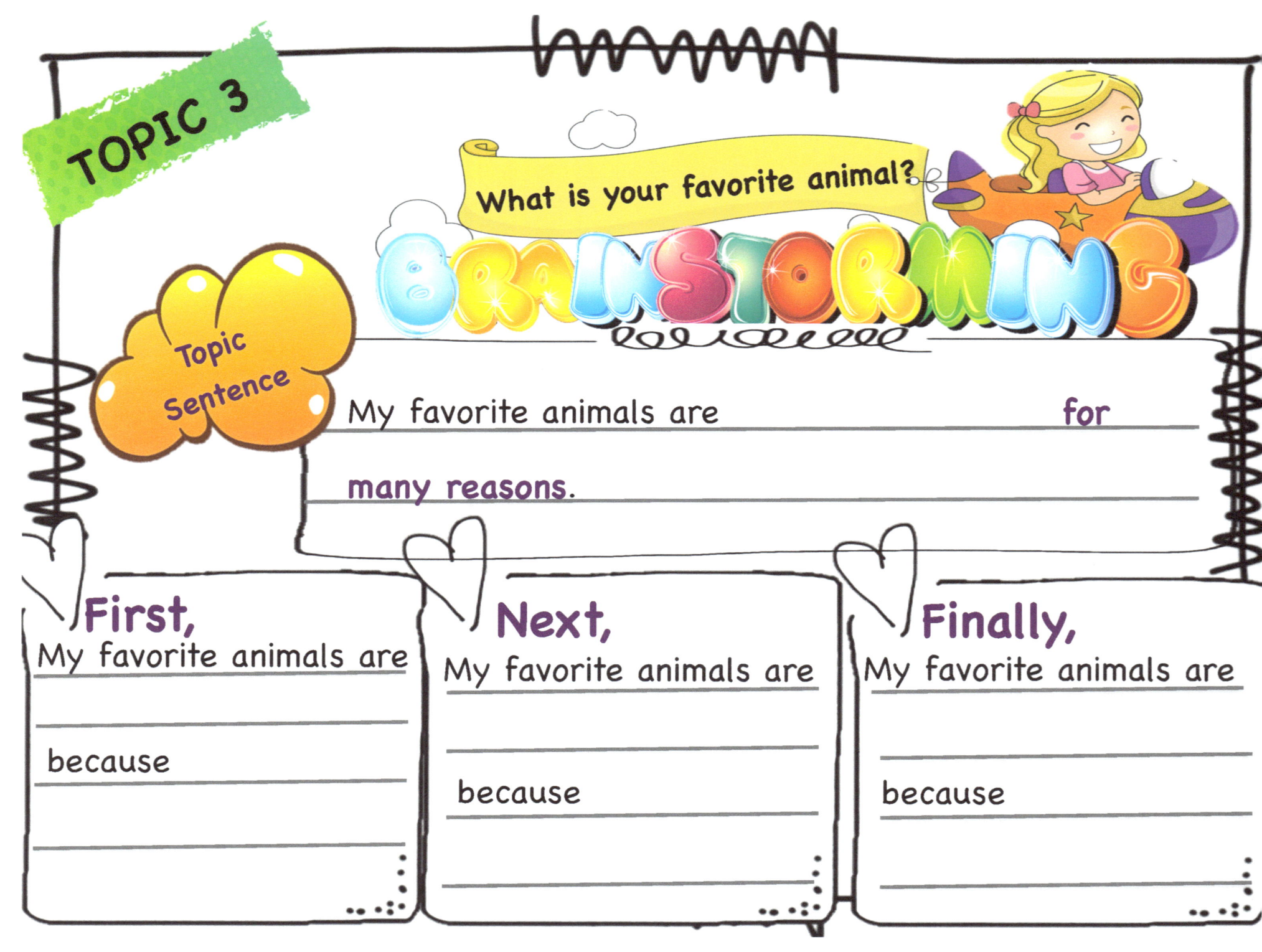

TOPIC 3

Use your paragraph to draw pictures.
(Show each of your reasons.)

FIRST,

NEXT,

FINALLY,

TOPIC 4

Use your paragraph to draw pictures.
(Show each of your reasons.)

FIRST,

NEXT,

FINALLY,

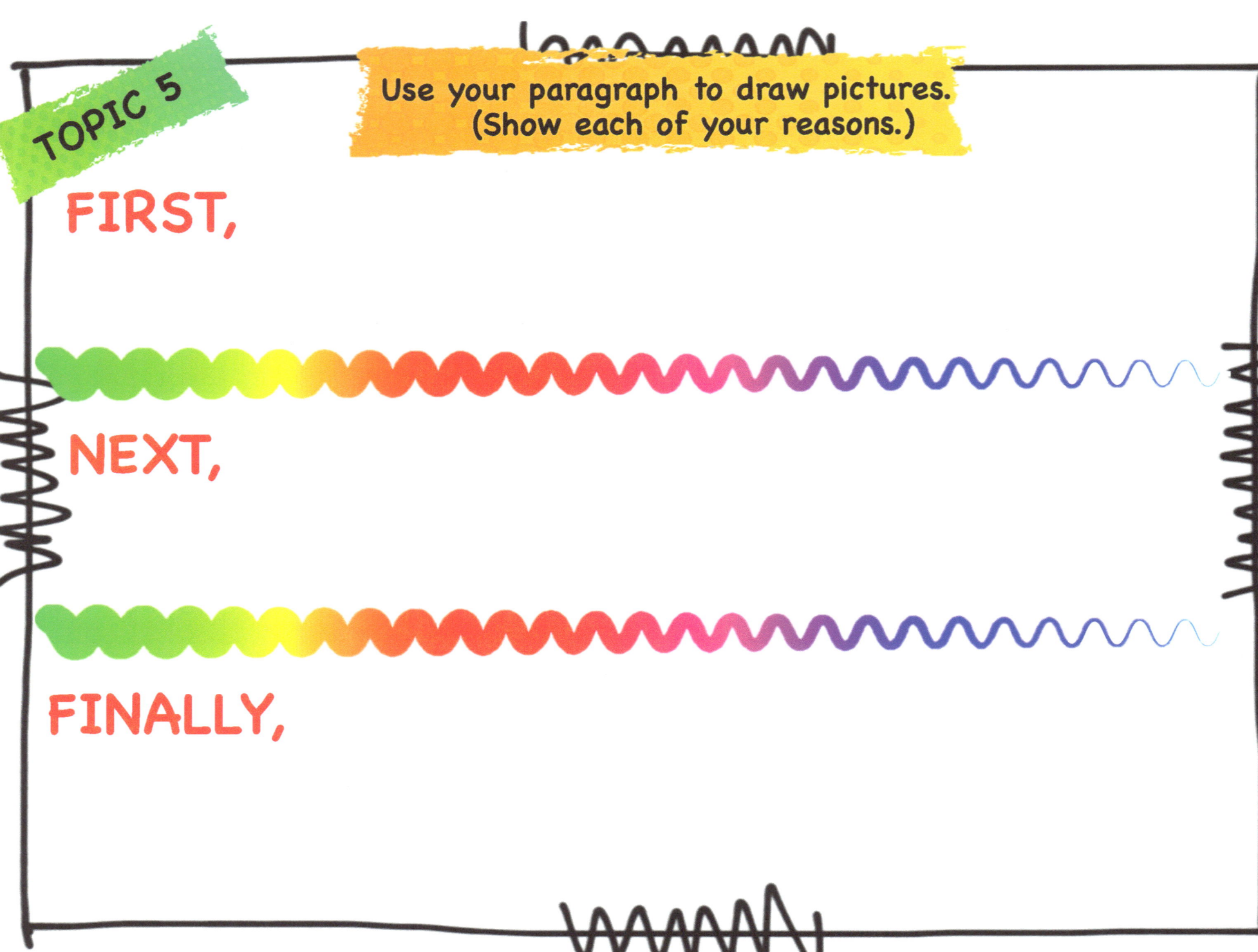

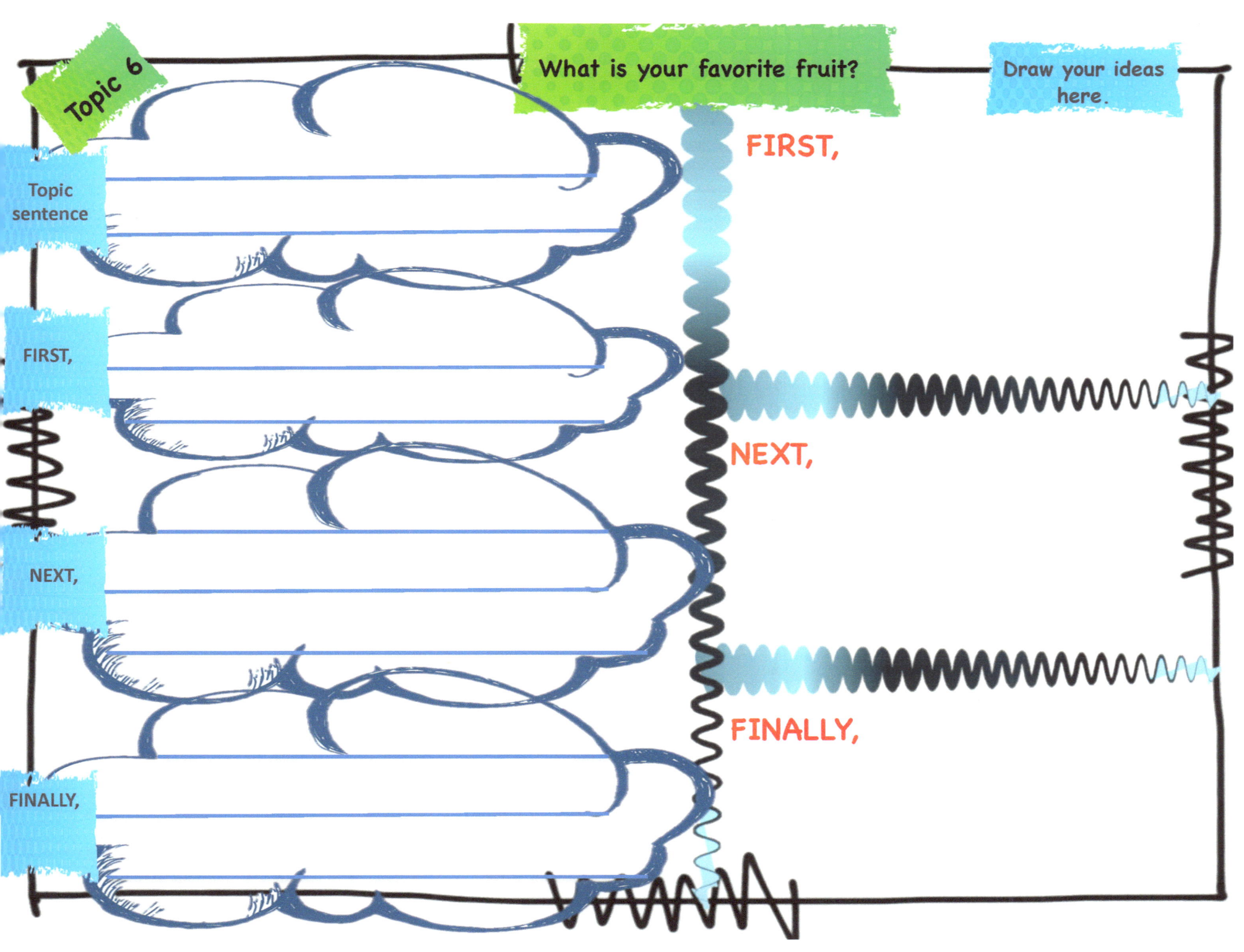

PART 2

Choose the best example.

Color A, B, or C.

My favorite animals are camels for many reasons. First, my favorite animals are camels because they have beautiful eyelashes.

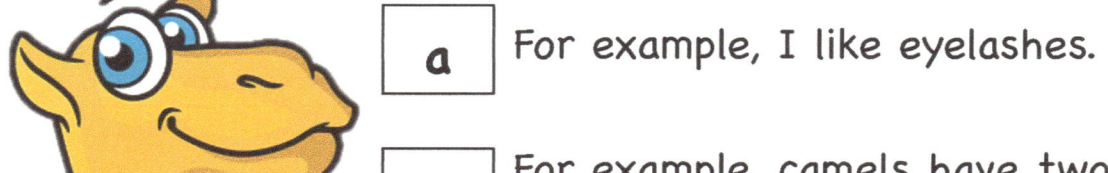

- [ ] a For example, I like eyelashes.
- [ ] b For example, camels have two rows of eyelashes that make their eyes look beautiful.
- [ ] c For example, camels live in the desert.

Next, my favorite animals are camels because they are strong.
For example, many people in the desert ride camels because they are so strong!
Finally, my favorite animals are camels because camels are herbivores.
For example, they eat lots of desert plants. But, they don't eat meat.

Put the paragraph in order. Write 1, 2, 3, 4, 5, 6, or 7 in the box next to the sentence.

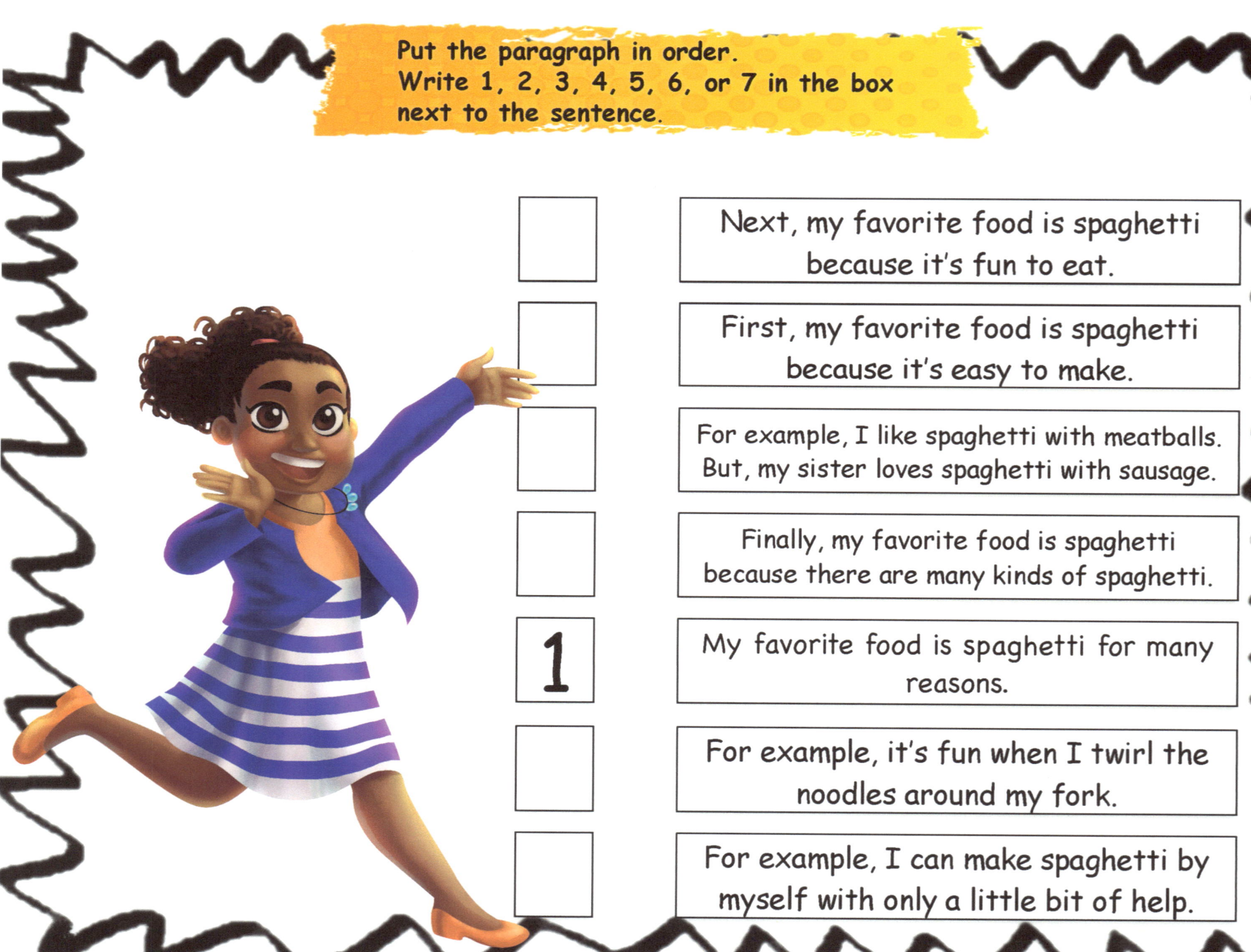

☐	Next, my favorite food is spaghetti because it's fun to eat.
☐	First, my favorite food is spaghetti because it's easy to make.
☐	For example, I like spaghetti with meatballs. But, my sister loves spaghetti with sausage.
☐	Finally, my favorite food is spaghetti because there are many kinds of spaghetti.
1	My favorite food is spaghetti for many reasons.
☐	For example, it's fun when I twirl the noodles around my fork.
☐	For example, I can make spaghetti by myself with only a little bit of help.

Put the paragraph in order. Write 1, 2, 3, 4, 5, 6, or 7 in the box next to the sentence.

1	My favorite place to play is my room for many reasons.
	First, my favorite place to play is my room because it's big.
	For example, I always clean my room very well after I play.
	Next, my favorite place to play is my room because it's always clean.
	Finally, my favorite place to play is my room because it's safe.
	For example, my bedroom is the 2nd biggest room in our house!
	For example, my room is safe because it's in my house where everyone loves me.

Topic 7

Do you need help with ideas?
Try these ideas or think of your own.

- because it is delicious
- because it tastes great with everything
- because it's fun to make
- because it is a special dish
- because we can buy it almost everywhere
- because I like to help my mom make it

- For example, it has lots of different flavors
- For example, sometimes I eat it with pie, sometimes I eat it with cookies, and sometimes I eat it with nothing else
- For example, when you make it, you can mix lots of different snacks in it
- Whenever my mom makes it, I pretend we are on a cooking show

TOPIC 7

"For Example"

What is your favorite dessert?

Topic sentence: My favorite dessert is _____ for many reasons.

Detail 1: First, my favorite dessert is _____ because it is delicious.

Example: For example, I think it's delicious because it tastes like _____

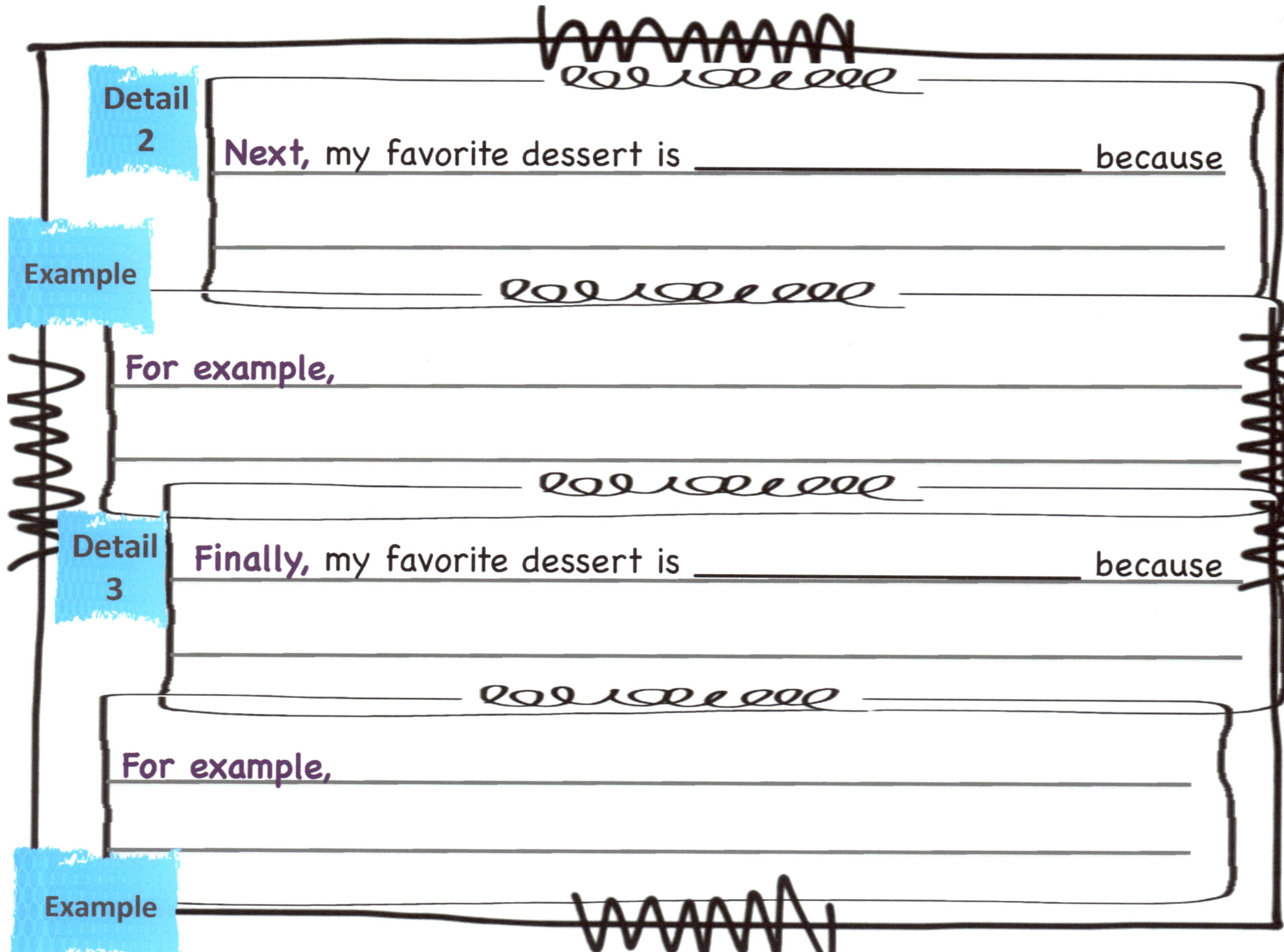

DRAW

Use your paragraph to draw pictures.
(Show each of your reasons.)

FIRST,

NEXT,

FINALLY,

Topic 8

Match.

Connect the reasons with their examples.

- My hands help me make things.
- My hands give me the ability to help others.
- We can use our hands to talk.

- For example, if someone doesn't understand me, I can use my hands to show what I'm saying.
- For example, I use my hands to make things out of clay.
- For example, I help my mother to carry things and I need my hands to do that.

TOPIC 8

"For Example" — What is your favorite BODY PART?

Topic sentence: _____

Detail 1: _____

First, my favorite body part _____

Example:

For example, _____

Detail 2

Next, _____

Example

For example, _____

Detail 3

Finally, _____

Example

For example, _____

DRAW

Use your paragraph to draw pictures.
(Show each of your reasons.)

FIRST,

NEXT,

FINALLY,

Topic 9

**Do you need help with ideas?
Try these ideas or think of your own.**

- because I have more free time on this day.

- because I can sleep late.

- because I can play with my best friend on this day.

- because I have ballet practice on this day.

- because my mom or dad comes home early on this day.

- because it is "Gym Day" at school.

- because I go somewhere special on this day.

- For example, I don't have to go to school the next day. So, I don't wake up early.

- For example, my dad usually comes home after dinner. But, on this day, he has dinner with us.

- For example, "Gym Day" is only once a week on Mondays.

- For example, I go to church with my grandmother every Sunday.

- For example, I don't have homework on Fridays. So, I can play more.

- For example, my best friend comes to my house every Thursday after school.

- For example, I have ballet practice every Tuesday and Thursday and it's so fun!

TOPIC 9

"For Example"

What is your favorite day of the week?

Topic sentence

_____

Detail 1

First, my favorite day of the week is _____ because _____

Example

For example, _____

Detail 2

Next, _____

Example

For example, _____

Detail 3

Finally, _____

Example

For example, _____

DRAW

Use your paragraph to draw pictures.
(Show each of your reasons.)

FIRST,

NEXT,

FINALLY,

Topic 10

Do you need help with ideas?
Try these ideas or think of your own.

- because it makes beautiful music.
- because you can play many different kinds of sounds with it.
- because it's the kind of instrument rock stars play!
- because I'm learning how to play it and it's so much fun.
- because it's really loud and I love loud music.
- because I like to watch other people play it.
- because it looks very interesting.
- because playing this instrument is great exercise for our brain.

- For example, many famous singers play the piano in their songs because it has a nice sound.
- For example, some piano keys are loud and some are very soft. They each make different sounds.
- For example, I have piano practice 3 times a week.
- For example, all instruments help us to exercise our brains when we play them.
- For example, I love really loud dance music that has drums!
- For example, it is fun to watch people play the piano. It looks like their hands are dancing.
- For example, when people play the harp, they look like angels!

TOPIC 10 — "For Example"

What is your favorite instrument?

Topic sentence:

Detail 1:

First, my favorite instrument is the _____ because

Example:

For example,

Detail 2

Next, _____
_____
_____

Example

For example, _____
_____
_____

Detail 3

Finally, _____
_____
_____

Example

For example, _____
_____
_____

DRAW

Use your paragraph to draw pictures.
(Show each of your reasons.)

FIRST,

NEXT,

FINALLY,

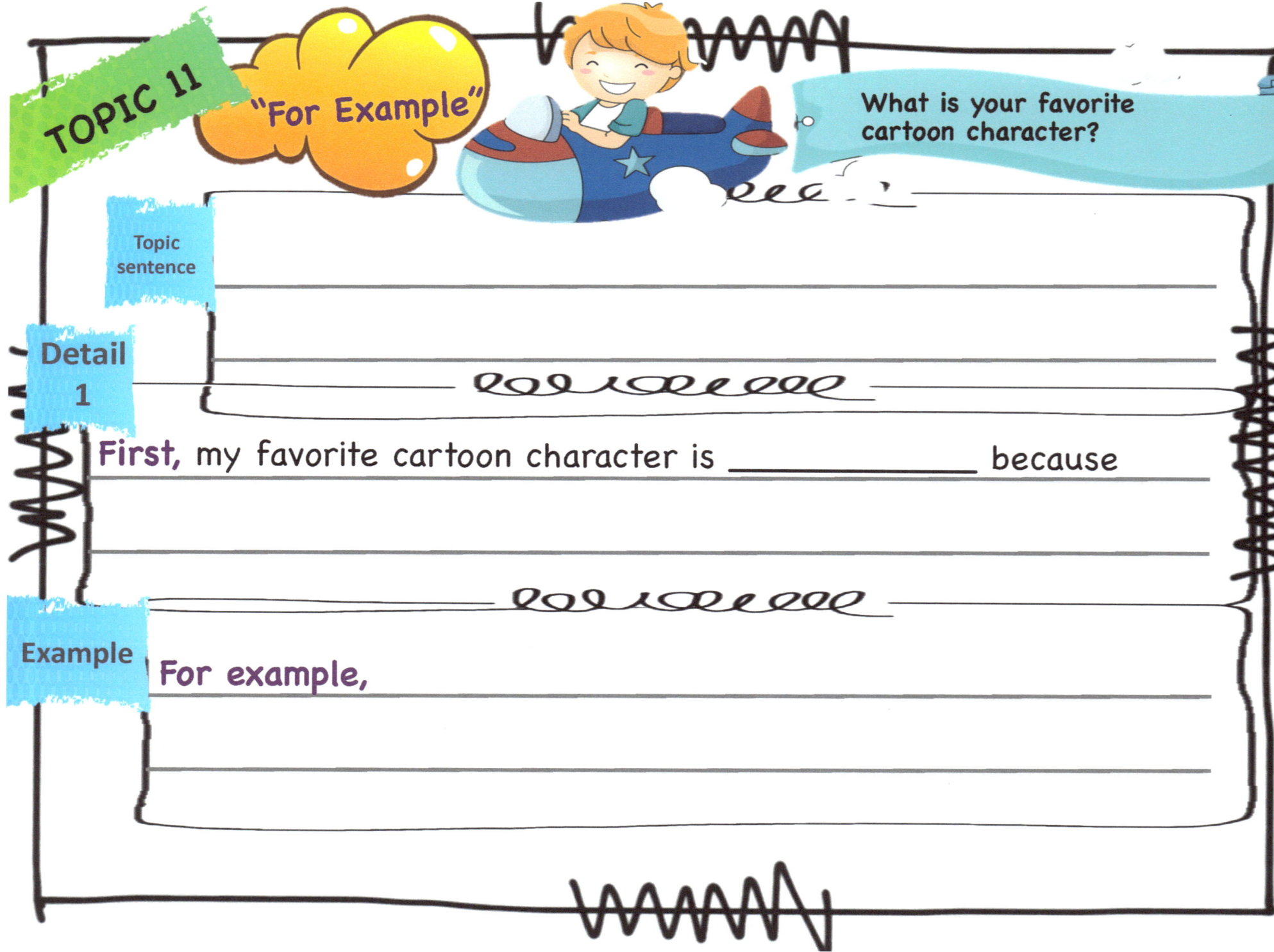

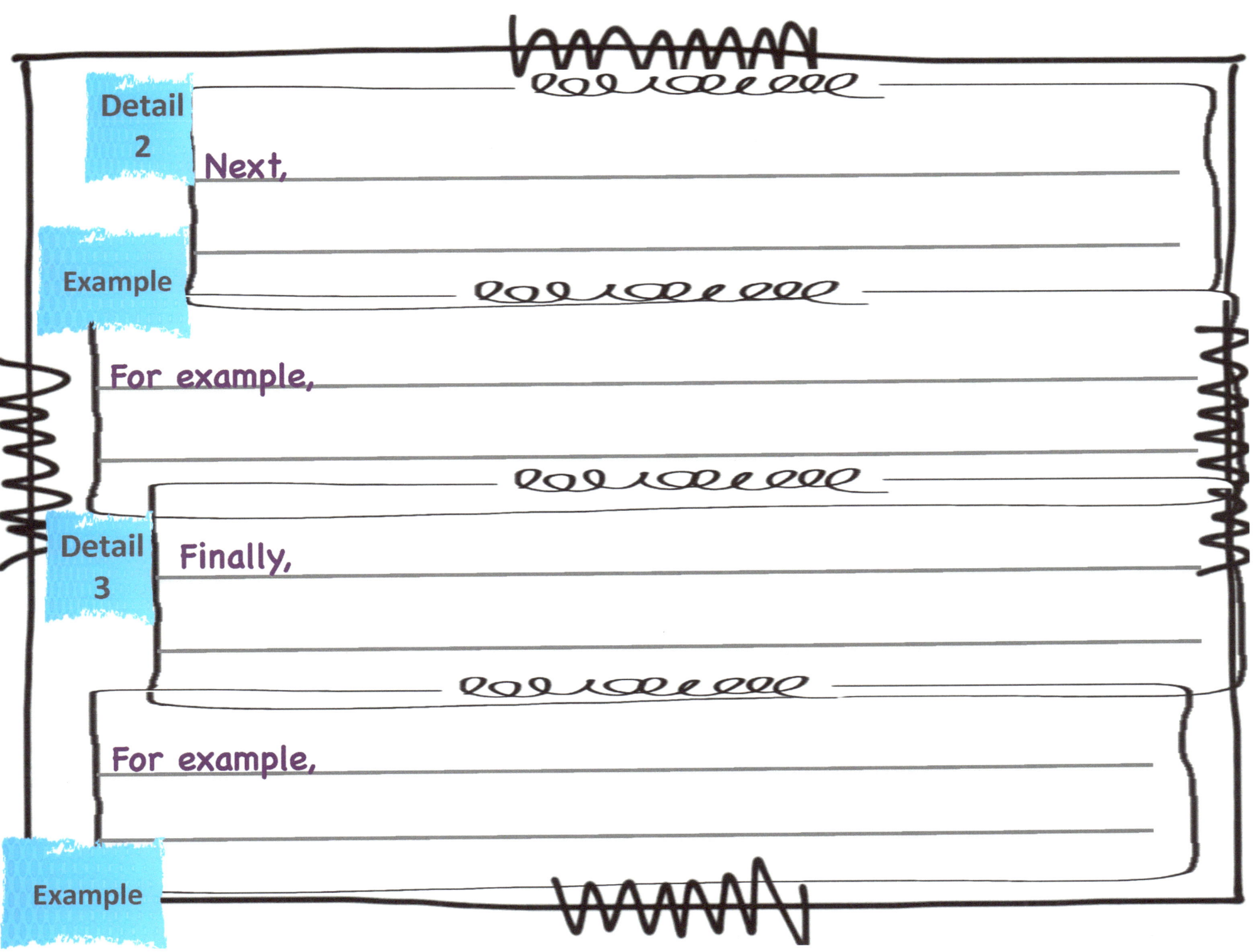

DRAW

Use your paragraph to draw pictures.
(Show each of your reasons.)

FIRST,

NEXT,

FINALLY,

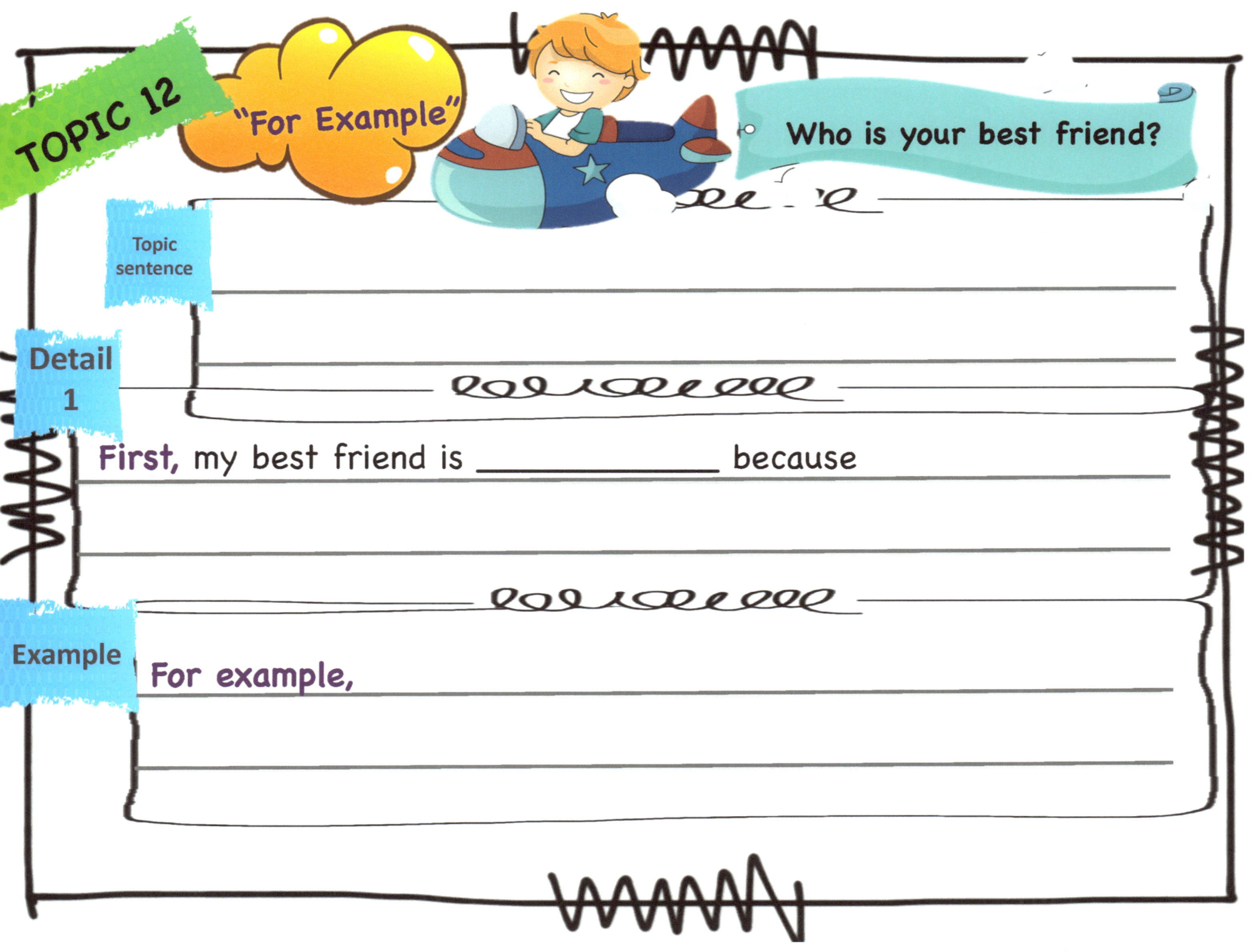

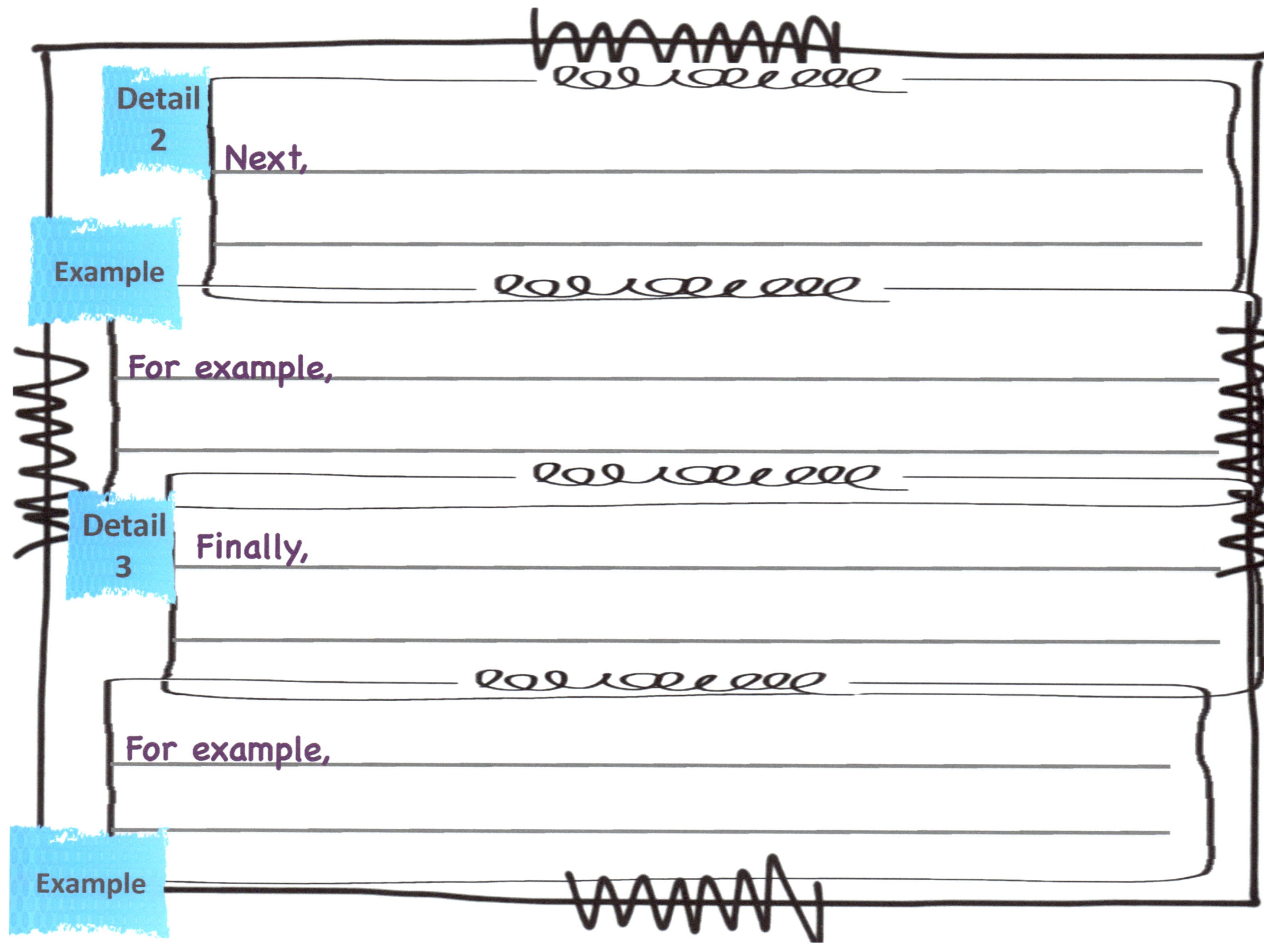

DRAW

Use your paragraph to draw pictures.
(Show each of your reasons.)

FIRST,

NEXT,

FINALLY,

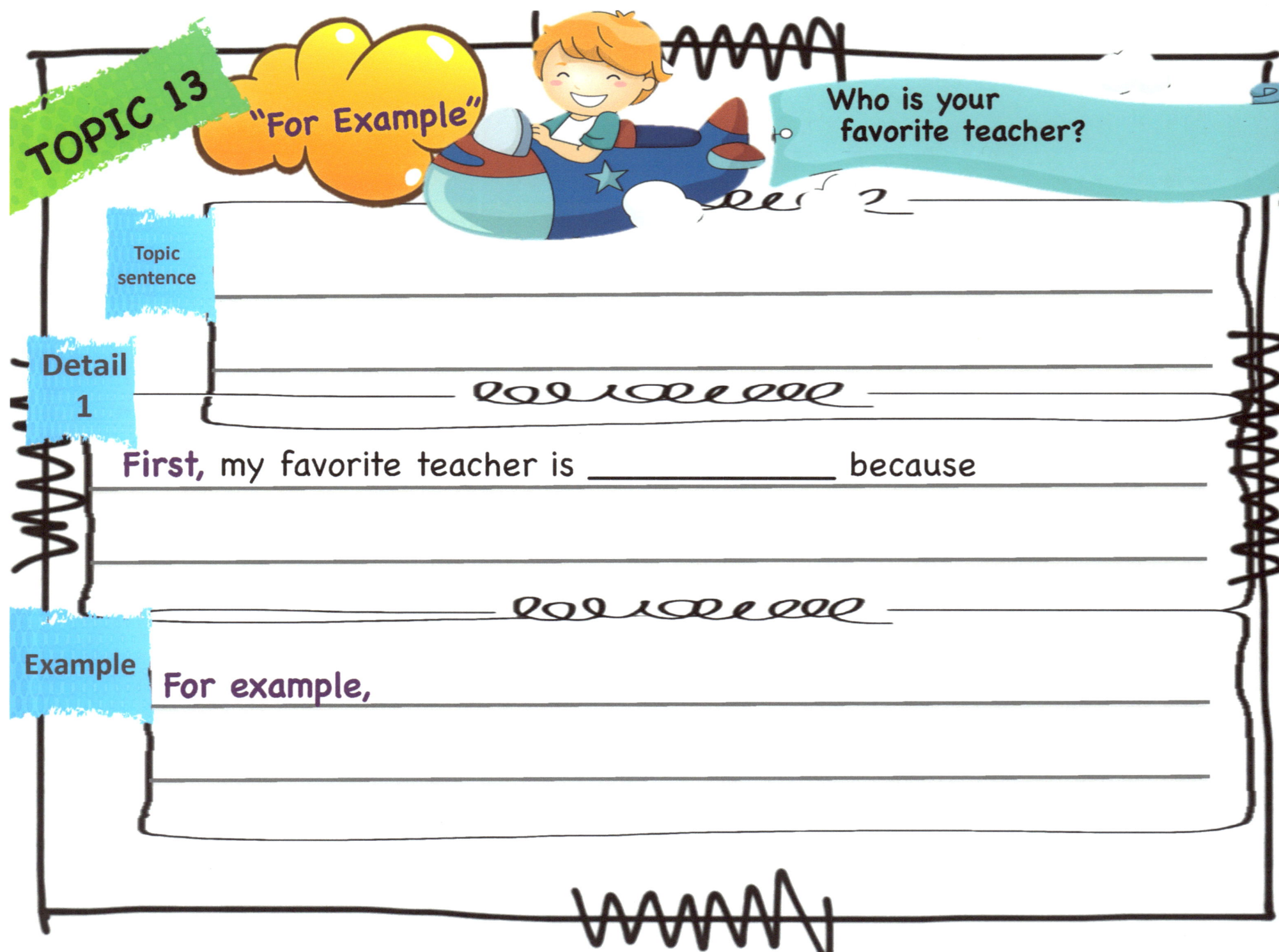

TOPIC 13 — "For Example"

Who is your favorite teacher?

Topic sentence

Detail 1

First, my favorite teacher is _____ because

Example

For example,

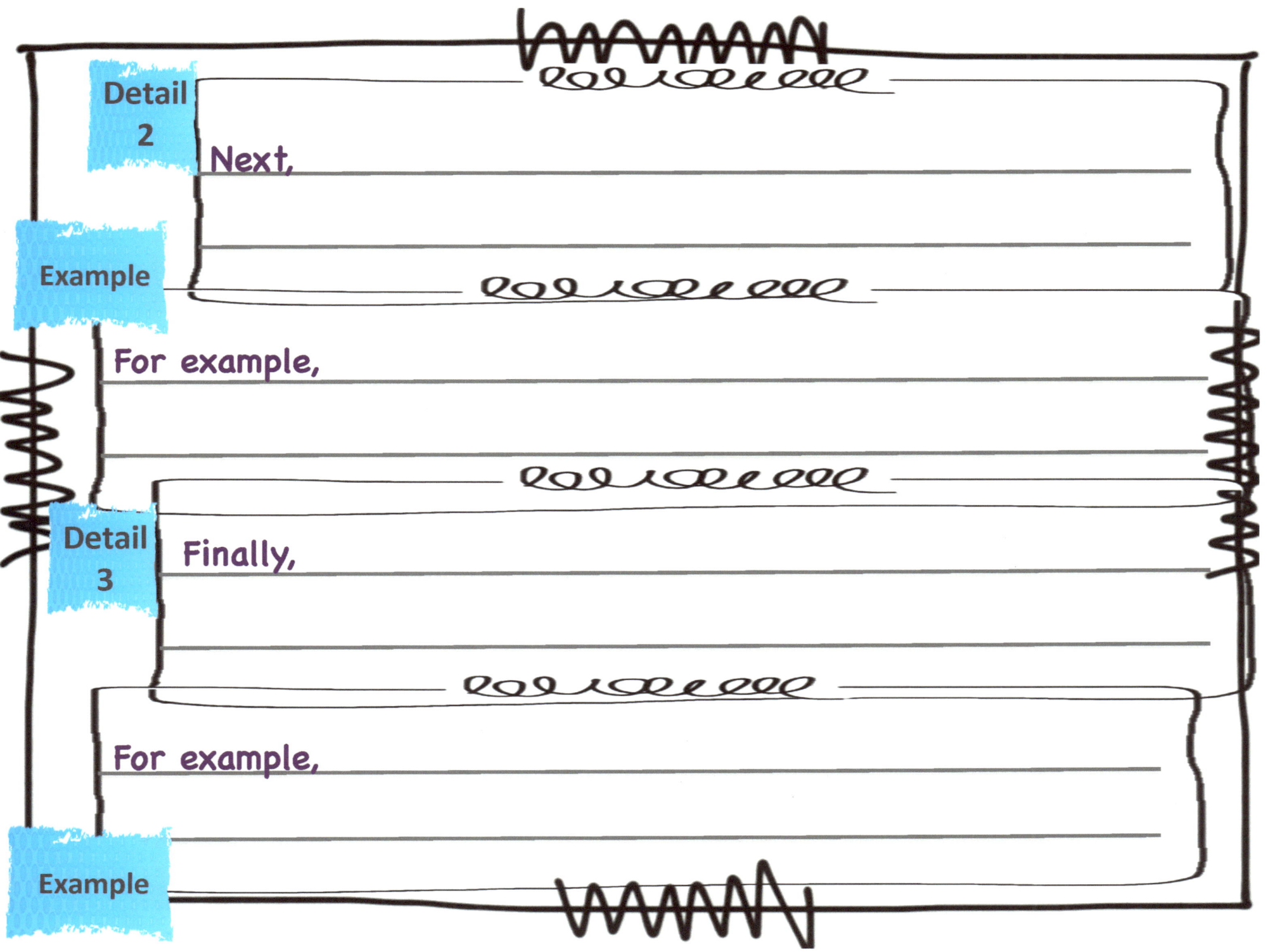

DRAW

Use your paragraph to draw pictures.
(Show each of your reasons.)

FIRST,

NEXT,

FINALLY,

TOPIC 14

"For Example"

Who is your favorite person?

DRAW

Use your paragraph to draw pictures.
(Show each of your reasons.)

FIRST,

NEXT,

FINALLY,

CELEBRATION TIME

How will you celebrate?

Today, I will

_____

_____

because I did a great job and I learned to write a paragraph by myself! sign: _____

www.kidYOUniversity.com

www.ingramcontent.com/pod-product-compliance
Lightning Source LLC
Chambersburg PA
CBHW041153070526
44584CB00004B/290